EYE ILLUSIONS ™

Written by Jim Anderson
Book Design by TXF Graphics

Modern Publishing
A Division of Unisystems, Inc.
New York, New York 10022
Printed in the U.S.A.

INTRODUCTION

Welcome to a new world! Hidden within the beautiful abstract pictures in this book are exciting three-dimensional images. All you need to do is look at the pictures in a special way, relax, and the images will unfold in front of you as if by magic. You will see images of animals and toys, people and things — all in brilliant color and sharp detail. You might even be tempted to reach out and touch them.

The wonderful images in this book are called "stereograms." They are flat, two-dimensional pictures that, when viewed in the right way, appear to have three dimensions. Early 3-D pictures were really two images, and you needed special glasses or a special viewer to look at them. Thanks to modern computer technology, stereograms are now single images that can be viewed directly by anyone!

For hundreds of years, scientists have been studying how vision works. Artists began using this knowledge to draw 3-D pictures over 150 years ago, but since they drew by hand, it took them a long time to create even one image. The development of computers changed everything. Starting in the 1960s, artists used computer graphics to create ever more complex and beautiful 3-D art. At first, the 3-D images were simple shapes and designs. As computer graphic technology improved, and as the artists grew in their craft, more detailed and exciting pictures were created.

We can see these pictures in three dimensions because all human beings have "binocular" vision. Our eyes are several inches apart, so each eye sees things from a slightly different angle. This information is combined in the brain to give us a 3-D view of the world. Things not only have height and width, they have depth as well. Stereograms, though they look like simple abstract patterns, actually contain all the information the brain needs to "see" a 3-D image. The information for the right eye is on the right side of the picture, and that for the left eye is on the left side. By relaxing the focus of our eyes, we allow the two sides to overlap, and the brain is "tricked" into seeing a 3-D picture. It's a simple idea made possible thanks to complex technology. Truly, these 3-D pictures show us a new world!

INSTRUCTIONS

To see these 3-D images, you need the right setting. First, find a quiet place with bright lighting, and make sure the picture you look at is evenly lit. Then sit up straight, take a deep breath, and relax. This is very important. The more relaxed you are, the easier it will be to find the images, and the more fun you will have. Also, be patient, especially in the beginning. It may take several minutes before you can see the picture in

three dimensions. So take it easy and don't give up.

There are several ways of viewing the 3-D images in this book:

Method One

Begin by looking at the cover picture. The cover is shiny, and you should be able to see your reflection, or the relection of a light in it. Look at the picture on the cover, but focus your eyes on the reflection. This will make your eyes relax and go out of focus. Stare at the picture for a minute or two until you "feel" something start to happen. Just relax, continue staring, and the 3-D image will appear.

Method Two

Another way to see the 3-D image is to bring the picture right up to your nose. Don't try to see the image — just let your eyes go completely out of focus. Then, while keeping your eyes out of focus, move the picture back to about arm's length. Keep looking at it with your eyes relaxed, and after a little while, the 3-D image will "pop" out.

Method Three

A third approach is to try and "see through" the picture. Look at the page, relax your eyes, and imagine you are looking "beyond" the book. Keep looking for a few minutes. Remember, patience is important. So is relaxation. Just take it easy and enjoy yourself. In time, a beautiful 3-D image will appear to you.

These three methods make up the "parallel-viewing" technique. There is also a "cross-eyed" technique that is more comfortable for some people.

Method Four

To view the images in the cross-eyed way, bring your finger, or a pen or pencil, up close to your eyes. Focus on the finger, pen or pencil. As you hold this focus, look at the stereogram. It may take a few minutes, but the 3-D image will appear. Once you develop one technique, try to develop the other. Sometimes, different techniques allow you to see slightly different images in the same stereogram. For example, if you look at a 3-D image of birds flying in the sky, the parallel-viewing technique may show you the birds in front, with the clouds in the background. With the cross-eyed technique, however, you may see the clouds in front, looking as if the birds have already flown through them leaving bird-shaped holes!

There are 14 images in this book, each with a riddle to help you discover what it is. If you're patient and keep at it, you will soon be able to see all of them. Then you truly will be an expert in the world of 3-D!

Opposite: *Have you ever watched workers put up an office building or apartment house? Then you've seen this machine in action. When people are building things, they use it to push all the dirt they dig into a big pile. It's very noisy and makes a lot of smoke.*

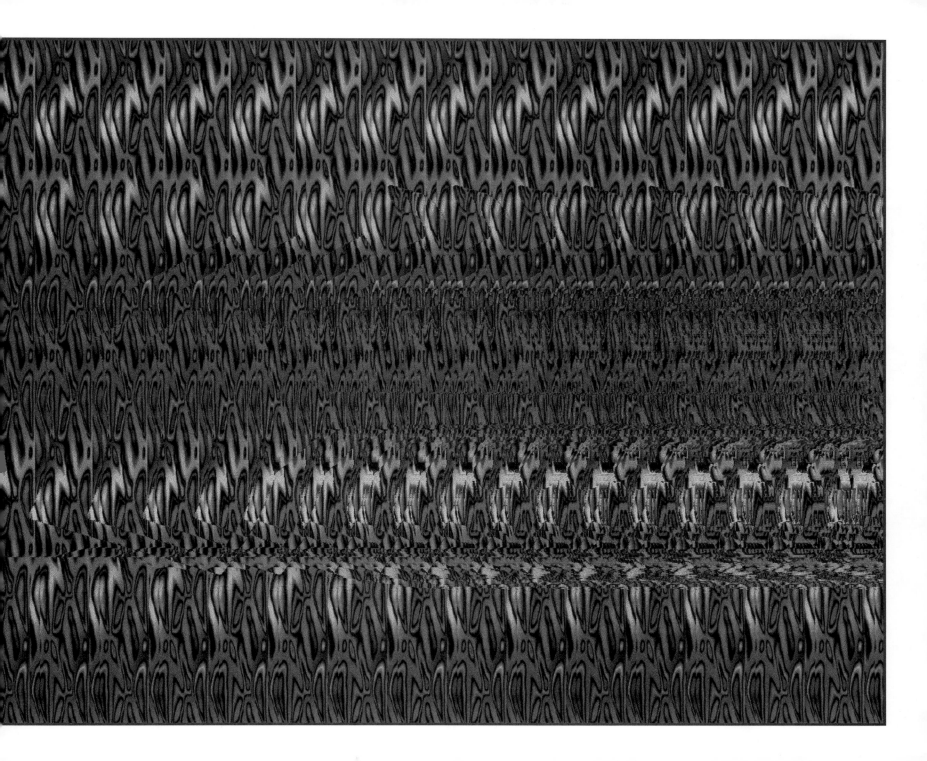

Farmers use this building to store food for their animals. It's a wonderful place to explore on a rainy day. You can lie in the hay and straw, pet the horses and the other animals, and look at the farm tools. You may even want to move in!

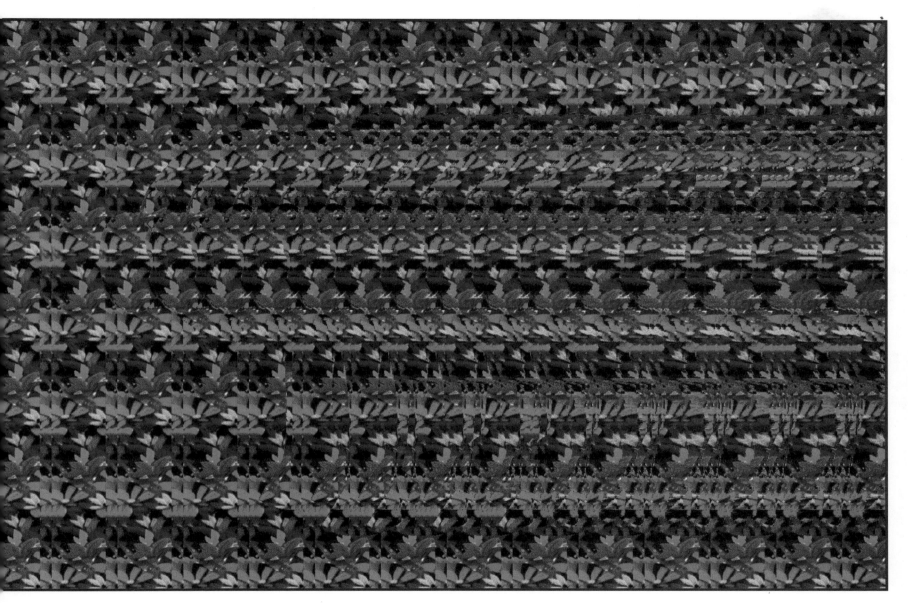

I have a corkscrew, but I don't open bottles with it. I'm happy and friendly, but nobody keeps me as a pet. You'll see me and all my friends if you go to the country and visit a farm. I love to eat, so bring me an apple if you come to say hello!

You see him at the circus balancing on a ball. He's large and furry, with big teeth and claws, but he's really friendly if you don't tease him. He likes nothing better than a tasty fish dinner, with some berries and honey on the side. Yum!

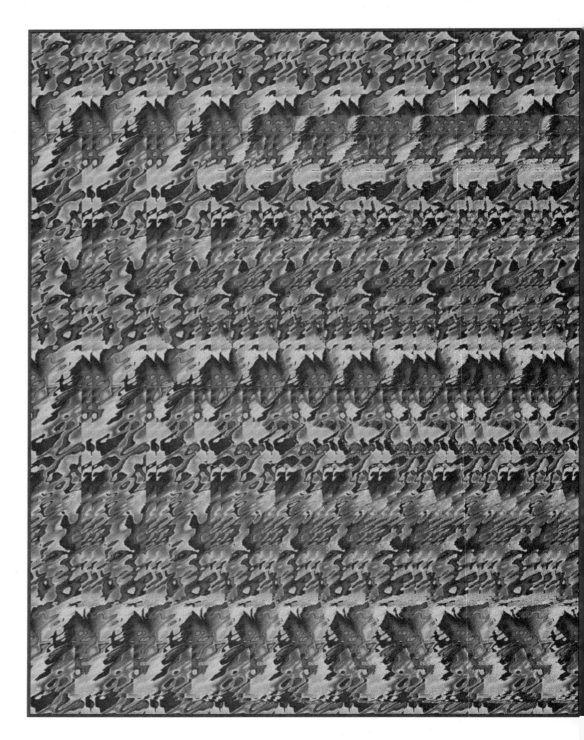

Presto! This is a magician's favorite trick. First it's empty, then it's not! How do you think it's done? Maybe if you practice really hard, you can learn to do the trick, too. But remember, you have to take good care of the animal.

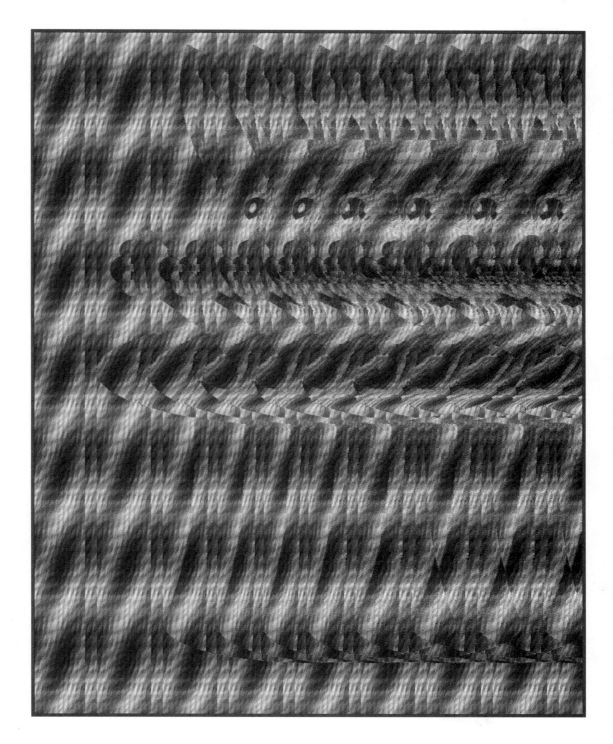

Look up! You'll see this among the clouds, taking people from city to city, and from country to country. It's the best way to travel! You may know someone who's been on one, and maybe you have been, too. So, hop on board and get a bird's-eye view of the world.

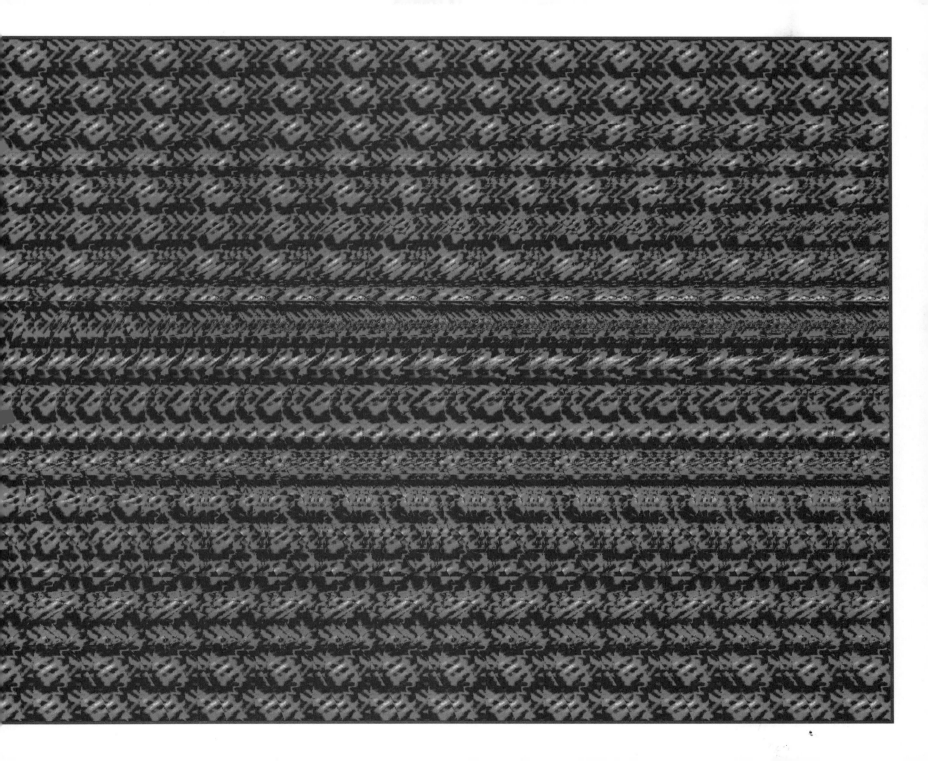

Opposite:
Girls love to play with these and sometimes boys do, too. Big or small, fancy or simple, they are a favorite toy in every family. Some are so old, they have been handed down from grandmother to mother to daughter. Some are even in museums. But most are in their own house.

Overleaf:
Boom-da-da-boom! That's the sound this makes, and it's LOUD! Soldiers play on this and so do rock stars. Maybe you have one at home. Just don't play late at night when everyone is trying to sleep!

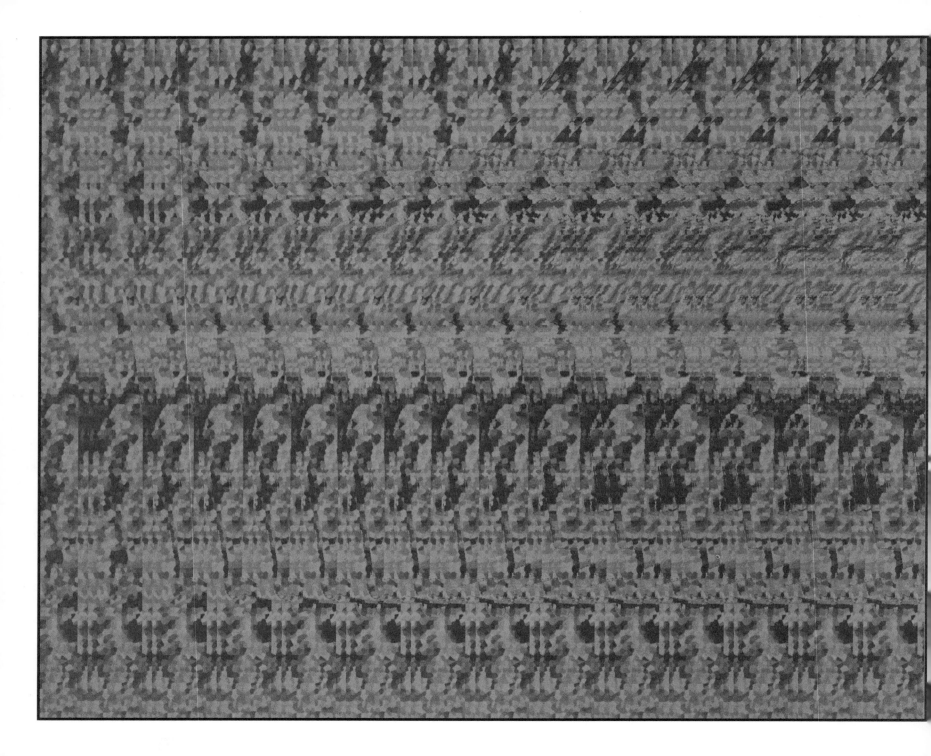

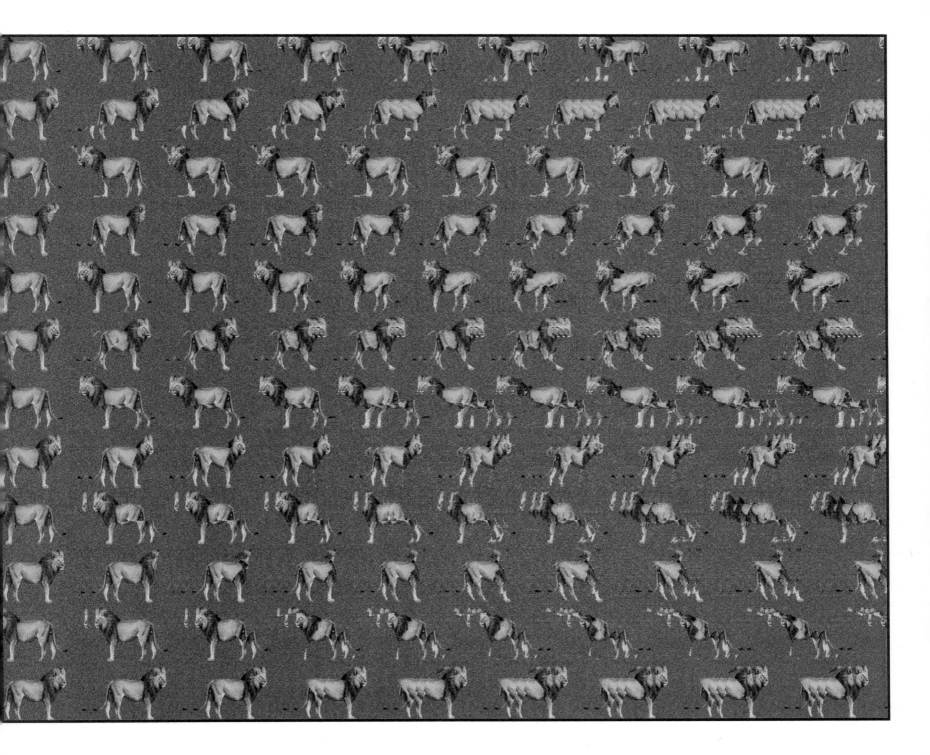

Previous page:
Everyone calls him the King. He lives in the jungle and is the ruler of all the animals. He's big and strong, but he's fair to everyone, and he loves his family. Maybe you've seen him at the zoo. He's easy to spot because of all the fur around his head.

Opposite:
You won't see this big fellow on the city streets! He lives in the northern woods among the pines and the fir trees. He's not mean, but he enjoys being by himself, and he likes nothing better than a good meal of grass and flowers. Look at his head and you can tell how old he is.

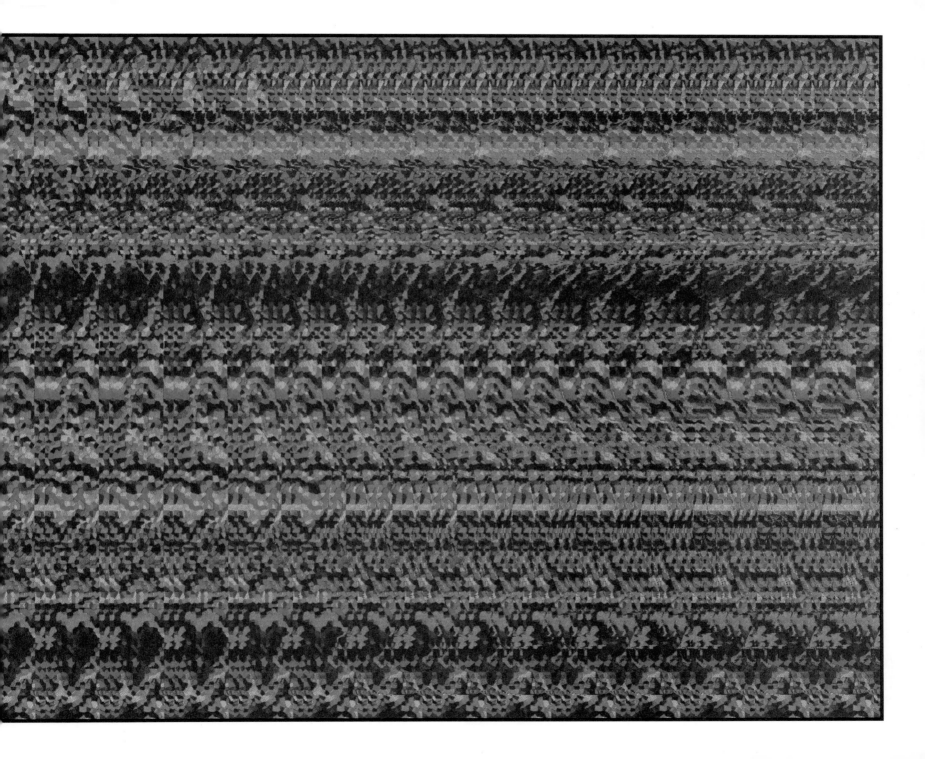

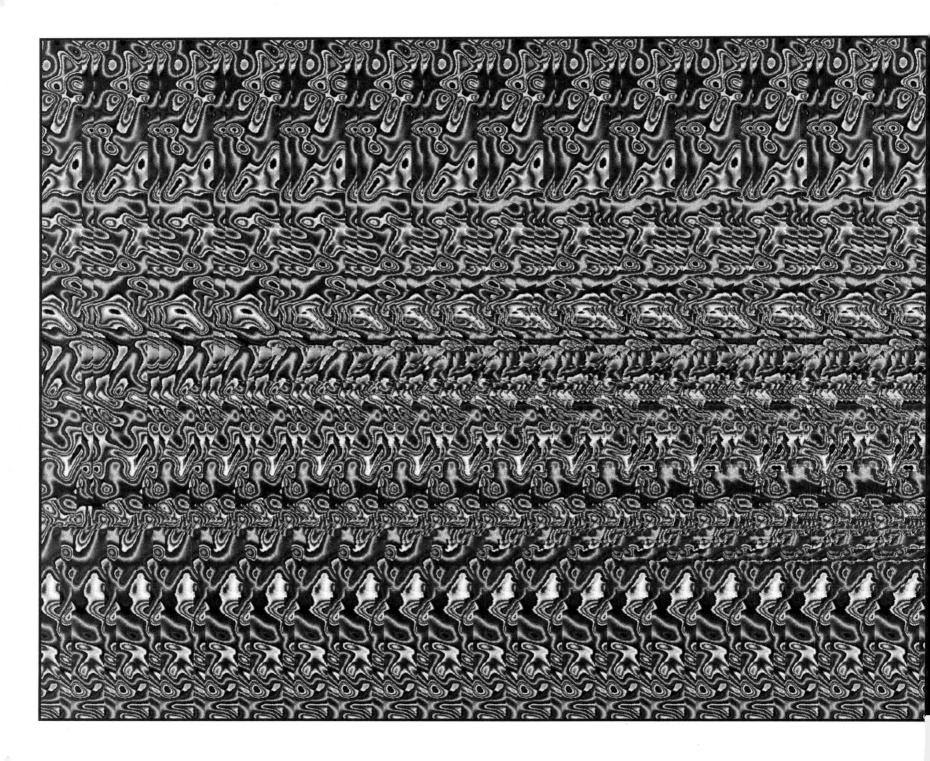

Opposite:
Toot! Toot! If you're lost at sea on a stormy
night, you'll be happy to hear that sound.
This boat does all the hard work and, even
though it's small, it can move big ships
into their docks. It's little, but it's strong.
Do you know what it is?

When you were little, this was probably your favorite toy. It's soft and furry, and always makes you feel warm and safe. Maybe you took it to bed with you every night. Did you know this toy was named after a president of the United States?

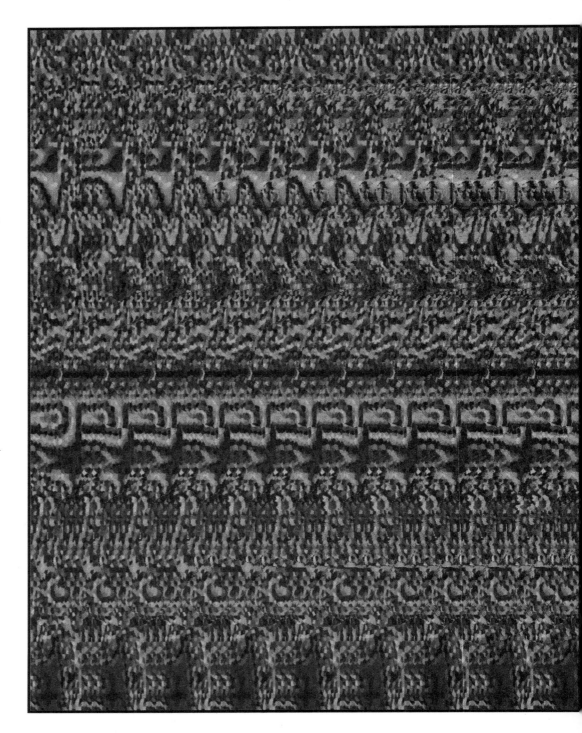

Here's a bird that loves to stick its "nose" into everything! But don't go looking for it in your back yard. It lives in the rain forest where the weather is always hot and humid. No snowstorms for this bird! It's motto is: "Two can" live as cheaply as one!

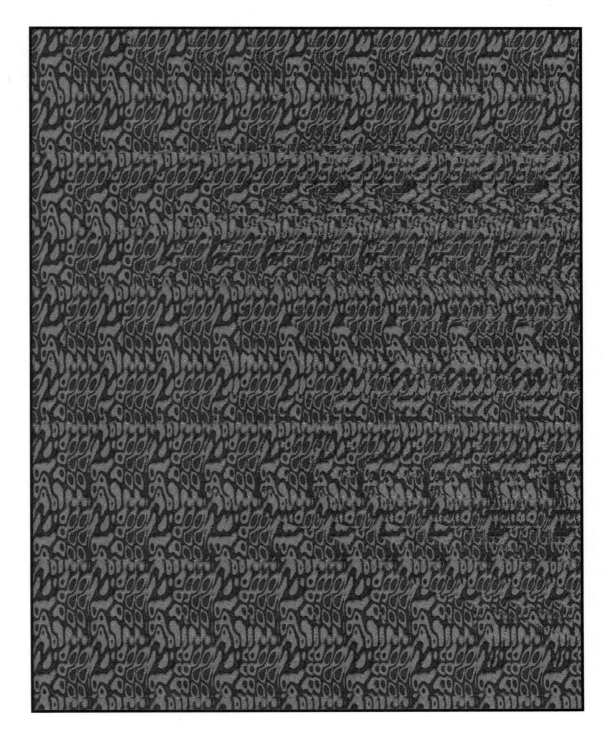

They're back! These animals disappeared a long time ago, but you can still see them on TV and at the movies, and everyone loves them. Some are as big as elephants. Others are as small as a pet dog. Some are really mean, but this one wants to be your friend. Go ahead and pet her!

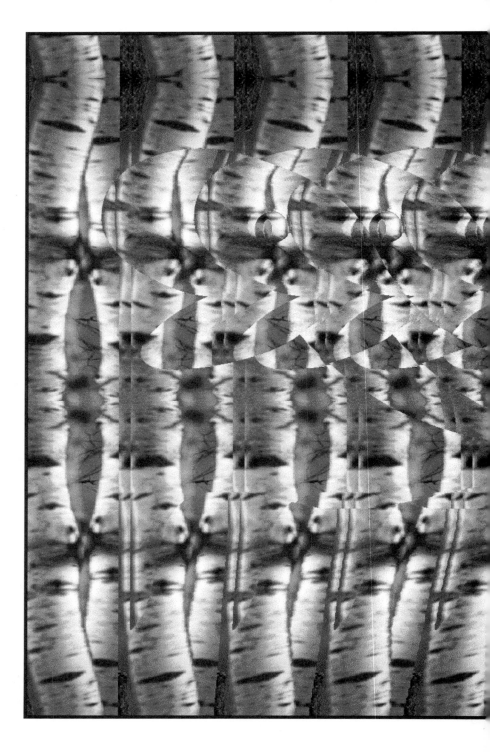

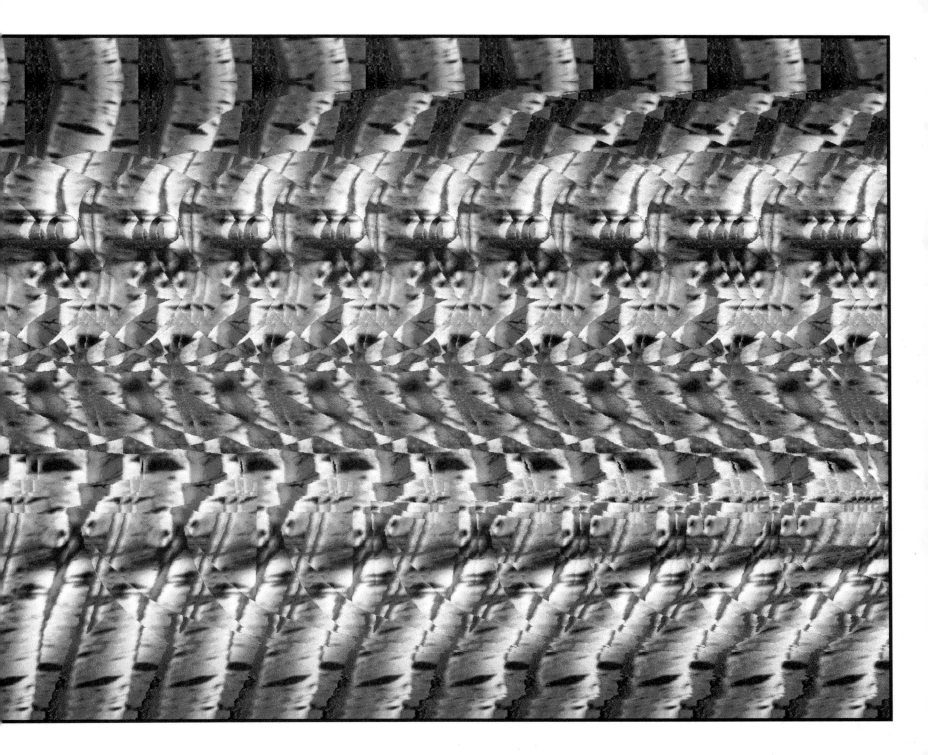

Page 5   Bulldozer

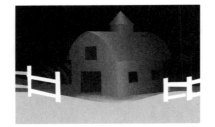

Page 6   Barn

Page 7   Pig

Page 8   Circus Bear

Page 9   Rabbit in a Hat

Pages 10-11   Airplane

Page 12   Dolls

Page 14   Drums

Page 15   Lion

Page 17   Moose

Page 18   Tugboat

Page 20   Teddy Bear

Page 21   Toucan

Pages 22-23   Dinosaur